# WHICH WAY ARE YOU LEADING ME, LORD?

**Bible Devotions for Boys**

## NATE AASENG

**AUGSBURG** Publishing House • Minneapolis

**WHICH WAY ARE YOU LEADING ME, LORD?**
Bible Devotions for Boys

Copyright © 1984 Augsburg Publishing House

Scripture quotations unless otherwise noted are from the Holy Bible: New International Version. Copyright 1978 by the New York International Bible Society. Used by permission of Zondervan Bible Publishers.

Photos: Jean-Claude Lejeune, pp. 10, 40, 66; Jim Cronk, p. 14; Norma Weinberg, p. 36; Jack Hamilton, p. 62; Leo M. Johnson, p. 88; Ron Meyer, p. 92.

**Library of Congress Cataloging in Publication Data**

Aaseng, Nathan.
   Which Way Are You Leading Me, Lord?

  ( Young readers )
  Summary: A collection of Bible devotions for boys including stories that present a problem accompanied by appropriate scripture texts, discussion, action ideas, and prayers.
  1. Boys—Prayer-books and devotions—English.
[1. Prayer books and devotions.  2. Boys—Conduct of life.
3. Christian life]  I. Title.  II. Series.
BV4855.A2    1984      242'.62      84-21562
ISBN 0-8066-2113-3

Manufactured in the U.S.A.          APH 10-7099

    3  4  5  6  7  8  9  0  1  2  3  4  5  6  7  8  9

# WHICH WAY ARE YOU LEADING ME, LORD?

# Contents

# About This Book

Wouldn't it be simple if every morning the phone would ring and God or one of God's secretaries would explain your assignments for the day? Then, once a year, God could sit down with you and map out what lies ahead in your future. You might still have trouble doing what God wanted, but at least you'd know exactly what was in store for you.

Of course, it's not that easy. We don't have a detailed map of what is ahead of us. The very mention of the word *future* to boys your age can make your heart skip a beat. Your mind is all clouded, confused by conflicting statements from friends, school, family, church, news, TV, and advertising. You may get totally opposite advice from two different people.

So where does that leave you? God is leading you, but *where* is he leading? The answers in the Bible are sometimes as confusing as all the rest of the answers in your life. It seems the Bible can give two completely different answers to the same question. We're supposed to change and stay the same, stir up action and bring peace, make noise and keep quiet. How do you make sense out of that?

This book is an attempt to clear up some of the confusion. Think of driving a car along the highway. Where do you steer? One answer is that you have to stay to the right of the center line. But if that were the only answer, you could just as easily drive into the ditch on the side of the road. So there is a second answer—you must stay to the left of the ditch. Steering both to the left and the right may seem like opposite instructions, but you have to do both to stay on the road.

The message of the Bible often works the same way. It lets you know where the boundaries are, what to watch out for and what to steer between. There is enough room between God's guidelines so that you can live a very different life from another boy, and yet both of you are following where God is leading you.

This book won't give you a detailed look into your future, but my hope is that it may help you to follow the Leader into the most exciting and challenging life possible.

# 1  You Are Special . . .

*"Are not five sparrows sold for two pennies? Yet not one of them is forgotten by God. Indeed, the very hairs of your head are all numbered. Don't be afraid; you are worth more than many sparrows."*

*Luke 12:6-7*

God knows everything about you, right down to the number of hairs on your head! That's not always a pleasant thought. It can make us think of God as a security officer who tracks our every move and thought. Like the song about Santa Claus, we can picture God as having a thick file on all the times we've been bad or good.

But Jesus didn't say these words so that we would be scared into behaving. He used them as a way of showing how much God cares. With God, it isn't a case of "if you've seen one human, you've seen them

all." God loves to keep up on how his creatures are doing.

Our minds can't work that way. We usually notice only those things that stand out from the crowd. We pay money to see rare animals in zoos but don't give a second glance to a plain old sparrow. Crowds of people, too, are often faceless blobs to us. So when we find ourselves in a large crowd, a big church, or a bustling city, we can't help but feel unimportant. We don't stand out.

God, though, doesn't get overwhelmed by numbers. Millions of sparrows have flown over the earth, yet God could tell you stories about each one of them. There are billions of people in the world, yet God could write a book about each one of us. God cares enough to share our tiniest joys and our greatest heartaches.

Sometimes it seems that we don't count for much in this world. But God tells us that we are a valuable part of his world, that we're special enough to be worth his time.

John let a cluster of people pass so that he could slow down to read the poster on the bulletin board at church. He felt drawn to read it every time he passed by, even though he had it memorized. The poster advertised the father-child banquet, and it practically guaranteed a good time for all. The thing that always grabbed his attention was the notice that a pro football quarterback would be there. For a second, John pictured himself shaking hands with a real star quarterback, and then he turned and trudged down the hall.

*It's just like all that stuff in the store windows,* he thought gloomily. *Always in front of me, but I know I can't ever have it."*

He recalled the words *father-child* as they had been branded in purple on the poster. As usual, the only picture that came to mind was a TV commercial of a kid fishing, with his dad's arm around his shoulder. John had never felt that arm, not that he could remember anyway. Now he would have to miss the banquet because there was no one to take him.

Too depressed to enjoy the bright sunshine, John sat on the cement banister outside the church, waiting for his mom to finish talking with her friends. People streamed by and car engines roared to life, smiles and chatter surrounded him. John felt like he wasn't even there, or that he was a fly or a dried leaf that nobody ever noticed.

Mom was the last person out the door, along with an older couple, the Baldwins. John slid off the rail and walked towards the car.

"Say, John, could you do me a favor?" asked Mr. Baldwin. John turned and squinted back into the sun's glare. "You know I don't have kids at home anymore," Mr. Baldwin continued. "I was asking your mom if I could borrow you for a night. I'd really be proud to have a boy like you for my

12

son. Would you come to the banquet on Thursday evening with me?"

John hardly knew how to get the words out as he accepted. He slid into the car seat and looked back at the church door, and for the first time he thought that a little of that place belonged to him.

**Action Idea:** Find out the names of some people you don't know who are in your church. If your church has a pictorial directory, you can use that to get the names. Help those people feel special by saying "hi" and using their names.

*Thank you, Lord, for picking me out from the billions of people on earth, for watching out and caring for me. Help me to be happy with the way you've made me, and help me to find a use for the special talents you've given me.*

# 2 . . . But Not Number One

*"If anyone wants to be first, he must be the very last, and the servant of all."*

*Mark 9:35*

Everyone needs to feel important, but sometimes we get carried away. Jesus' disciples were caught showing off on at least one occasion. Something inside them made them want to grab others and say, "Hey, look at me! Aren't I something!" Before long they were arguing about which of them was the greatest disciple of all. Tempers and voices must have risen as each told about how much better he was than the others.

Our world is full of people who demand that they be noticed and admired. Advertisers are not shy about telling us how wonderful their products are.

Sports teams jab fingers in the air to tell everyone that they are number one. Children love to be the first on their block to do or have something, and parents boast about the children they have raised.

Jesus' answer to this is the same one he gave to the disciples back then. In God's eyes, there is more honor in putting others ahead of you than in trying to climb over them to the top. We don't have to prove to God or to others that we're better than all the rest. God doesn't love us because of our talent, looks, or brains, but simply because we are his.

He doesn't ask us to put others first because he likes to embarrass us. Rather, it's part of his plan to help us live as we should. God wants us to be so sure of ourselves and of his love that we don't have to always outdo each other. Rather, he would like us all to help others to be better off. That way, instead of number ones, number twos, and losers, there would be room at the top for everyone.

Jim felt so good he could have cartwheeled all the way home from school. "Look at that, would you?" he chuckled, waving a sheet of paper in front of Greg and Nick. "I got every single question right on the math test. One hundred percent. Just call me genius."

Greg pushed the paper out of his face. "Big deal."

"Oh, yeah? When's the last time you got everything right on a test?" Jim demanded.

"I've done it lots of times," Nick said, kicking a pebble off the sidewalk. "I could have done it

16

this time, but I just didn't feel like studying that hard for it."

"Who cares about math, anyway?" said Greg. "If you think you're so great, whose science project was put in the display case by the front door? You two couldn't even get yours to work."

Jim felt the blood rush to his cheeks. "Well, if you had had a klutz like Nick for your partner—"

Nick turned to him angrily. "Look who's talking! Who slipped and fell flat on his face doing the shuttle run in the gym today? I could have crawled and still beaten you."

"That's nothing," Greg said. "Mr. Perry told me that I set a school record for pull-ups last week. You guys couldn't even do four."

"That's just because you're such a shrimp, there's nothing for you to lift up," sniffed Jim, who felt ready to smack either one of his friends. They had ruined the walk home. "It's not fair," he thought. "I just got a perfect score; a guy shouldn't have to get cut down for that."

After half a block of awkward silence, Nick began to laugh. "Boy, there's no chance of anyone getting a big head around this group!"

The laughter popped Jim's cloud of bad thoughts. He remembered that other boys had laughed when he had fallen during that shuttle race, but those two hadn't. He also guessed that Greg really was disappointed by his poor score on the test.

"Aw, let's just say I had a good day," he said, folding the paper into his back pocket.

**Action Idea:** Try to think of ways that you can put others ahead of yourself. Serve the dessert to your family at supper and serve yourself last. Start clearing the table before anyone else does. Let others take a turn at a game before you do.

*Help me, God, to remember that the important question is not "How am I doing?" but "How are we doing? Don't let me get carried away so that I take pride in something that you have done through me.*

# 3    Strict Rules . . .

*Then he said to them all: "If anyone would come
after me, he must deny himself and take up his cross
daily and follow me.*

*Luke 9:23*

Uh-oh! You knew there had to be a catch. In trying
to show God's love, most of our Christian books and
lessons show smiling, happy faces. But being a
Christian can't be as easy as skipping down the
sidewalk. Deep down, we all know that if we want to
follow Jesus, we may end up doing some things that
we don't like. In this verse, Jesus lets us know that
this is true.

There's a popular highway sign that says, "55
miles per hour; it's not just a good idea, it's the law!"
In the same way, when God calls us to follow him,

he's doing more than giving out hints of what we might want to do. God has given us commandments, and he has made it plain that they are to be obeyed. We are to love God, our neighbors, and justice, to turn the other cheek, and stop being selfish. It may not always be our first choice of what to do. But if we follow God, we need to trust that he knows what is best. God doesn't expect perfection, of course, but he wants us to work hard to follow the rules.

People are not thrilled by rules. Somehow rules seem threatening, and we're afraid they will cut down on our freedom. But rules are really just a plan to help you reach a goal. If you want to lose weight, you must follow the rules of a diet. If you want to do well at a sport, you must follow a training schedule.

It's the same with following Jesus. The rules are there to help us. The more we work at following them, the more closely we can follow him.

The wrinkled, bony fingers stretched slowly toward the black game piece. After carefully lifting the piece, they rapped it down on another square of the board. "Gotcha!" said Mrs. Green, and she smiled as she winked at Kevin. "I finally beat you, you young rascal!"

Kevin nodded slowly; he had seen the end coming but hadn't been able to stop it. He looked up at his checkers partner and found he couldn't resist returning the smile. Mrs. Green had just turned 90, but she was a match for anyone when it came to checkers.

As he watched Mrs. Green struggle to get up from her chair to get them a snack, Kevin fought the urge to get it himself. He knew Mrs. Green was a proud woman who loved to wait on people whenever she could.

"There," she said, at last bringing a half-full glass of milk. "Just a minute and I'll get us some cookies. They're store-bought, you know. I'm afraid I don't bake anymore."

"Thanks for the snack and for the game, Mrs. Green," Kevin said as he opened the screen door. "We'll continue our battle the same time next week."

Tuesday night the phone rang. "Hey, Kevin, we're throwing a spur-of-the-moment party at my house for Danny tomorrow. He just moved in next door to us today. It's going to be a surprise and everyone's going to be there."

No sooner had Kevin hung up the phone than he remembered Mrs. Green. "Great timing! They had to hold the party right when I'm supposed to play checkers with Mrs. Green!"

Quickly he headed for his sisters' bedroom. "Can one of you do me a favor and play checkers with Mrs. Green tomorrow?"

Pam shook her head. "Cheerleading practice."

Kevin turned desperately to Gail, but she just frowned. "I wish I could help you, but I already arranged to go shopping with mom."

"Can't you change that?" he pleaded. Hearing no answer, he closed the door loudly and went to

21

his room. It wasn't that he minded playing games with the neighbor lady. But a party would be even more fun. He started downstairs to call Mrs. Green. "She can get along without me this once," he thought.

But he pictured that old face that brightened up when she saw him at the door. He knew how long the days were for her, how lonely she was. Although he didn't feel good about the choice as he set down the phone, he knew that the sight of Mrs. Green rubbing her eager hands together would make it seem worthwhile.

**Action Idea:** Think of something that you really don't *want* to do that you know you *should* do. Make up your mind to do it!

*O God, it's hard to think past right now. We're always tempted to do what will make us feel the best at this minute. Help us to trust your wisdom and to obey you, so that we will do what is best in the long run for you, our neighbors, and ourselves.*

# 4 . . . To Set You Free

*It is for freedom that Christ has set us free. Stand firm, then, and do not let yourselves be burdened again by a yoke of slavery.*

Galatians 5:1

There were early church members who were as suspicious of rules as we are. They didn't want anyone telling *them* what to do. They figured that if they had to follow orders all their lives, they were no better than slaves.

They probably thought that God's rules would lead to the kind of life common in the early days of our country. Some Christians frowned on entertainment, relaxation, or just about anything we might consider fun. Life was nothing but a long list of rules. These people thought that humans were naturally so evil that the only way they could stay out of trouble was by obeying all these grim rules.

But the book of Galatians tells us that we've got it all backwards. God's commandments won't make slaves out of us; they will make us more free than we ever were. God wants to save us from the miserable life that comes from living in sin.

Few criminals get their start in crime by suddenly deciding that's what they would like to do with their lives. Crime comes about when people are locked into bad habits, sinful surroundings, hatred, greed, and desperation. If only they could be set free from all that! Our world, too, seems trapped. Countries spend millions of dollars on weapons while millions of people go homeless and hungry. We don't want it that way, but we can't find a way to change it.

God's command to love can help us break away from the messes that sin gets us into. His way can help us to concentrate on being what we're supposed to be. What greater freedom is there?

"Think fast!"

Hearing the warning, Mike whirled just in time for the flying chalk eraser to hit him flush on the cheek. Bobby stood by the teacher's desk, laughing, while Mike angrily reached down to grab the eraser. The two of them had come back early after finishing their lunch and were alone in the room. All Mike could think about was getting even, and he flung the eraser at Bobby with all his might.

But Bobby was able to dodge it enough so that it just clipped his elbow. The eraser glanced off and hit a photograph and a vase of flowers on the teacher's desk. Bobby laughed harder than ever, but Mike wasn't thinking about him. Racing to the desk, he managed to whisk away the photograph before water spilled on it. But there was glass everywhere, both from the vase and from the picture. Mike picked up one of the carnations and then looked at the clock. The others would be back from the lunchroom in a minute or two. Dropping the flower, he bolted from the room with Bobby close behind him.

Mr. Trenton was scowling by his desk when Mike returned. Mike was glad he had remembered, at the last instant, to wipe the chalk off his face. As long as Bobby kept quiet, there was nothing to tie him to the crime. Still, whenever Mr. Trenton looked in his direction, Mike started to squirm.

Mr. Trenton finished his short, biting speech by saying, "What really disappoints me is that whoever did it doesn't have the nerve to own up to it." Mike started to feel sick.

It was worse the next day when Bobby came up to him with an awful grin. "Give me your lunch money or I'll tell Mr. Trenton," he said. Mike threatened to pound him, but in the end he had to hand over the money.

Mr. Trenton had been in a bad mood all day. By afternoon the pangs of hunger added to Mike's

25

misery. How many days could this go on? Mike tried desperately to see a way out of his problem.

Finally, with his head throbbing and stomach churning, he made up his mind to confess after school. He wasn't sure what he had expected from Mr. Trenton, but he found it wasn't as awful as what he had been going through all day. After Mike apologized, Mr. Trenton simply asked if he saw any way to correct the situation. Mike quickly agreed to pay for whatever was broken, the two shook hands, and that was that.

As Mike left the room, he felt like he was walking out of a jail. "Whew! Now I can go on living again!"

**Action Idea:** New Years Day isn't the only time for trying to break bad habits. Think of one habit you have that you would like to break. Then come up with a plan for doing it.

*Lord, I don't want to spend so much of my time ducking, dodging, and covering up the trouble I get into. Help me to realize that in following you, I will be more free than I could possibly be without you.*

# 5  Some Things Always Change . . .

*He who was seated on the throne said, "I am making everything new!"*

*Revelation 21:5*

When we think of people who are "stuck in their ways," we often think of older people. That's unfair, of course. Who is a bigger stick-in-the-mud than a one- or two-year-old child? An unfamiliar bed or a strange face can send the child into sobs. Many small children would throw a fit before they would dare taste a food they hadn't tried before. The fact is, we all fight change, from birth to death.

In the time of Christopher Columbus, many areas of the world were unknown to Europeans. Their mapmakers often drew sea monsters or dragons in these unknown corners of the world. Our view of the un-known hasn't changed much in 500 years. We know our world isn't perfect, but we'll usually accept it over the dreaded unknown.

As this verse shows, though, God is always push-ing for change. God is looking for better things from us, so he wants us to change, to grow. Although change is not always for the better, things *can't* get better *without* change.

Imagine if you still worked, played, and thought at the same level as you did in kindergarten. You would have missed out on a lot of life. Much as we dreaded new experiences and challenges at that time, we're sure glad now that we have gone through them. The thought of growing into new responsibilities may scare us now, but we'll be glad in years to come that we grew. We'll find, just as Columbus did, that the unknown isn't always filled with horror. It can help us grow so that we can do God's will better tomorrow than we did today.

Even though school was out for the year, Marc couldn't get it off his mind. This summer was all that stood between him and junior high. Every time he passed that sprawling, brick school build-ing, he broke into a sweat.

He had heard talk about that junior high. You had to change classrooms every hour, and the building was so big you could get lost. There were sometimes fights in the halls, and Marc had even heard that they made you take showers in gym class. Already he was feeling behind some of the

28

other boys in his class because he didn't have a girl friend. *I know I'm not going to do well in junior high*, he thought.

Normally a quiet guy, Marc had even started to avoid his own family in the last weeks. Every evening he slipped downstairs to the den, sank deep into the cushions of the corner chair, and watched TV. His mom made some comments about the time he was wasting, but he ignored them.

One night mom interrupted his show to say, "The family that moved in across the street seems to have a boy your age. You don't have many friends in the neighborhood. Why don't you go over and meet him?"

Marc didn't take his eyes off the TV. *Leave me alone*, he thought. *I've got enough problems. Just let me watch TV*. After a few seconds of fidgeting, he said, "What if I can't stand him? Besides, you know I'm no good at meeting people."

"You don't have to impress him. Just be friendly," answered his mom. "No one says you have to be friends, but you could give it a try."

Marc wished his mom would leave the room. Finally he pushed himself out of his chair, only because he couldn't think of a good argument against her.

Although it was well after supper, it was still hot, and Marc sped his bare feet quickly across the warm blacktop toward the house. When he saw the boy standing behind the open back of a van, he hesitated, then kept going.

"Hi, I'm Marc. I live across the street."

"Hi," grinned the boy. "I'm Darrel. Looks like we're about the same age. I'll be going into junior high next year."

"Yeah, me too. I hear junior high is really different."

"Hey," laughed Darrel. "Everything is different to me right now." He shook a stick of gum free from a pack and offered it to Marc. "Got any good bike trails in the neighborhood?"

"Sure, follow me." Marc felt proud to have a good bike trail to show him. He ran quickly back to get his bike. As he pulled it out of the garage, he thought, "That TV program was boring anyway."

**Action Idea:** Is there a skill, a craft, or a hobby that you have always thought looked interesting? See if you can get someone to teach it to you.

*Lord, it must get discouraging for you. For thousands of years you've tried to help humans change for the better, and we've dug in our heels and fought you every inch of the road. Move me so that I want to grow, and help my changes to be for the better.*

# 6 . . . Some Things Never Change

*Jesus Christ is the same yesterday and today and forever.*

*Hebrews 13:8*

This New Testament writer doesn't seem to be fired up about change. He is actually bragging that Jesus never changes. The church seems to join in this thinking when it talks about keeping the "old values." In fact, churches often fight hard against change in our society. Christian parents, too, often stick to some old-fashioned rules. Why?

Think of a group of hikers heading off into a wilderness. In a dense forest, it's easy to get twisted around without realizing it. Hikers need to have something that always stays the same in order to keep from getting lost. A compass can provide a good checkpoint to let them know if they're wandering off course. North is always north; it never changes. Hikers can count on that unchanging fact to keep them out of trouble.

In our lives, it's easy to wander into trouble. Our world changes so fast that sometimes what seemed wrong yesterday seems OK today. Selfishness and cheating can gradually seem to be just an ordinary part of daily life. Fortunately, God's law doesn't change with the times. His command to love and live honest lives means the same today as it did long ago. His Word is always there so that we can know if we are starting to slip away from God.

We can be glad that God's truth never changes. As long as we can keep it in sight, we know that we can grow and change without fear of falling away from God.

"I want you to remember this, because it's important!" barked the gymnastics teacher. "No one jumps on the trampoline without two spotters on every side! Jumping on the tramp may seem like fun, but it's also dangerous. So I don't care if you like the rule or not; if I catch you even sitting on the tramp without spotters, you're through!"

Jeff was surprised to hear such a speech from the coach. He had taken a class from him once before and had thought he was such an easygoing man. But the coach wasn't backing down on this point. "You two on that side, you two there, you two back there, and Jeff with me! Brad, go on up and take the first turn."

Jeff watched as Brad bounced higher and higher on the tramp. He wondered if it really was as dangerous as the coach made it seem. As the days passed, he began to have more doubts. Everyone was doing simple jumps, and no one even came within a couple of feet of the edge. *Why waste everyone's time?* he thought. *Even if you want to be safe about it, you could get by with four guys instead of eight.*

Brad was on the tramp again, trying a back flip. No problem. "Try it again," repeated the coach, and Brad did as he was told. "Again," said the coach. Jeff yawned and turned to look at the clock. Just a half hour left of this practice.

"Jeff! Pay attention! It's no good having you stand there if we can't count on you. We've got to have you ready every second that someone is on the tramp."

"I don't know what the big deal is," grumbled Jeff. He frowned until it was his turn. He hopped up on the tramp and began bouncing at once. It felt good to be flying so high, higher than any of the other boys could jump.

"Easy now, try the routine we worked on yesterday," said the coach. Jeff nodded as he bounced, then grabbed his legs and leaned backwards. Somehow, though, he landed at the wrong angle. Instead of springing back in the air, he shot forward and to the side. He knew that he was flying off the tramp, but he couldn't even tell which way was up. Then he felt the arms and the

33

mild jolt as he tumbled in a heap on top of someone.

"You OK?" the coach asked as Jeff tried to figure
out where he was. "You went into that a little out
of control. Good job, spotters. You want to get
back up and try again, Jeff?"

"On one condition," Jeff said, smiling weakly.
"That you never change your rule about spotters!"

**Action Idea:** Think of a person whom you can always count on when you need help. Let that person
know that you appreciate it.

*Thank you, God, for always being there. What a relief
it is for me to know that your love for me never
changes. Thank you for always being there when I
start to drift into fads or ideas that do not follow you.*

# 7  Forgive Us Our Sins . . .

*Here is a trustworthy saying that deserves full acceptance: Christ Jesus came into the world to save sinners.*

*1 Timothy 1:15*

There is a word that has caused medical doctors a great deal of dread over the years—*malpractice. Malpractice* is a legal word, and it means that a doctor may be held responsible if he makes a mistake while doing his job. Doctors are only human, and the best of humans make mistakes. All it could take is one wrong decision made in a split-second emergency, and the doctor could be in big trouble. The doctor could be sued for thousands of dollars and his or her career could be ruined.

The thought of a malpractice suit could cause a lot of worry for a doctor. So most doctors turn to

malpractice insurance. With this insurance, if a decision turns out badly, there will be enough money to settle any suit. That helps the doctor to go about his business without the constant worry that a mistake will ruin him.

We all face the same kind of pressure when we try to share God's love. We're all human and we all make mistakes. Sometimes we can cause tremendous pain by our thoughtless actions. If God demanded justice and ordered us to pay for all our mistakes, we would be ruined. There's no way we could pay. We could become so afraid of making mistakes that we wouldn't step out of the house.

God, though, has given us his own form of malpractice insurance. He sent Jesus into the world to keep us from being ruined by our mistakes. Jesus has guaranteed payment for our sins, so we can go on with our lives without fear of disaster. Doctors don't deliberately become sloppy or lazy just because they have insurance, and neither should we. But it is a comfort knowing that if we are really sorry for our sins, God will clear all the charges.

It had been a bad week for Pete. He couldn't leave his sister in peace, and his parents kept scolding him for his teasing. Then he completely forgot about a social studies assignment. Even before that, he had been doing poorly in that class. As he sat in Sunday school, he felt downright mean. He knew he had a nasty temper, and he could feel it slipping out of control.

The teacher mentioned that Pastor Wilson would be coming to their class next week. Randy then told a joke about the pastor to Pete, who laughed out loud.

"I don't think we need that in this class," said the teacher.

Pete backed down quickly. "Don't blame me. It's his fault," he said, pointing at Randy.

"Neither of you are behaving very well," the teacher said. "What is Pastor Wilson going to think?"

Pete's temper suddenly shot off, and he called the pastor a name. As soon as he had done it, he saw the class stare wide-eyed at him. He felt hot blood rush to his temples as he slunk lower in his seat.

"Perhaps you'd better leave," the teacher said wearily. Embarrassed by his outburst, Pete was glad to duck out early. But when he got home, his mother produced a scribbled note from her pocket. "What's this about a meeting with Pastor Wilson before church next week?"

Pete could feel his face going white this time. There was no hiding what had happened, so he told the details to his mom. She was near tears as he finished, and that made him feel worse.

"Come in and sit for a minute," Pastor Wilson said as he put on his robe for the service. "I hear you don't think much of me."

Too nervous to sit, Pete said, "Sorry, it was a mistake. I don't know what happened." He shrank back as if expecting a punch. *Anyone who could call a pastor that must be going straight to hell,* he thought.

"Then I guess you never called me that name," smiled the pastor. Seeing Pete's puzzled look, he went on. "You appear to be sorry about the whole thing. God says that's good enough. As far as he's concerned, if you're truly sorry, then it's as if it never happened. And if it's good enough for God, it's good enough for me."

"That's all there is to it?" Pete asked. "For something as bad as what I did?"

"Jesus forgave the people who killed him, so I hope I can forgive a slip of the tongue," he smiled.

**Action Idea:** You have a special chance to feel God's forgiveness during the church service. Be ready to confess your sins at prayer time. Use that time to confess your sins to God and to tell him that you really are sorry.

*Dear Jesus, I know that I have sinned. I really am sorry for (list any that you can remember). Also, some things I've done in the past still bother me (list any that apply). Help me to trust in your forgiveness.*

# 8 ... As We Forgive Those Who Sin Against Us

*Then Peter came to Jesus and asked, "Lord, how many times shall I forgive my brother when he sins against me? Up to seven times?" Jesus answered, "I tell you, not seven times, but seventy times seven."*

*Matthew 18:21-22*

Jesus must have had "forgive" at the top of his list of what he wanted us to do. In the prayer that he taught us to pray, the Lord's Prayer, he asked us to include only one promise: that we would forgive others. Each time we pray the Lord's prayer we are making that promise to him. How many times have you made that promise?

The idea of forgiving others is one of the strangest ideas that Jesus taught. It doesn't fit in with the idea

41

of justice—that people should get what they deserve. Almost everyone agrees that if you do good, you should be rewarded; if you do wrong, you should pay the price. If someone hurts us, our first thought is to make sure they feel at least as bad as they made us feel. It's called "getting even."

The disciple Peter believed in people getting what they deserved. He wasn't sure that he had heard right when Jesus talked about forgiving, about letting people off without punishment. That didn't sound fair. So Peter wanted to know how often Jesus would let someone do something wrong before he finally cracked down on him. Would he let this nonsense go on as many as seven times?

Jesus' answer must have floored him. "Seventy times seven," he said. That's a lot of forgiving! But Jesus used that number to get across the idea that we must learn how to forgive and do it often.

Larry dumped his schoolbooks on the counter top and bounced into the kitchen. He pulled open the refrigerator door and reached for the plate on the middle shelf. When his hand touched nothing but cold metal, he realized the pie was missing. A quick scan of the refrigerator told him that someone had made off with his dessert.

"What's going on?" he howled as he stormed onto the porch. There was his brother Dana reading the newspaper, with a glass of lemonade in one hand and the pie plate on the coffee table in front of him. Only one bite of evidence remained on the plate. "What are you doing? That's mine!"

42

Dana stopped eating and studied the remaining forkful as if seeing it for the first time. "You know, I had a feeling I shouldn't be eating this, but I couldn't remember why. This was yours from last night, huh?"

"Don't try to tell me you forgot! You heard mom say—"

"Honest, I just wasn't thinking. Here, want the last bite?"

"I ought to stick it in your face," Larry said. "I didn't eat any dessert at lunch 'cause I knew I could get some when I got home."

"I said I was sorry," answered Dana.

"This means war," fumed Larry. His chance came later that evening when they were doing dishes. As he was using the rinse hose to spray the glasses, he sent a quick burst into Dana's face.

"Cut it out!" yelled Dana.

"Huh? What happened? Did you get your face in the way of some water?" Larry sneered. "My hand slipped; it was an accident."

"Here's another accident," Dana said, as he swept Larry's books off the counter. The notebook flew open and paper fluttered everywhere.

Larry started to kick his brother, but Dana backed away. "You'd better be on your guard tonight, 'cause you're going to get it!"

"Plotting each other's destruction, are you?" asked dad, who had suddenly appeared in the doorway.

Both boys came at him at once with their accusations. Dad listened quietly and finally said, "So it all comes down to a slice of pie. If that's too big a problem to patch up, how are you going to make up after you've made each other good and miserable?"

After a moment of silence, Larry said, "I guess there's no sense getting into a war over some pie."

"A little forgiveness can save you from some serious hatred," said dad.

Dana turned to Larry. "I did say I was sorry."

"I know," Larry said. "It's OK. I should have known a dessert wouldn't last long in this house."

**Action Idea:** Is there someone you hold a grudge against for something that happened quite a while ago? Try to forgive that person, even if he or she doesn't seem that sorry. Also, when you find yourself getting into an argument, see what you can do to stop it before people get angry.

*Lord, I am promising to forgive every time I say the Lord's Prayer. Help me to keep that promise.*

# 9 Sometimes So Far . . .

*How long, O Lord? Will you forget me forever?*
*How long will you hide your face from me?*

*Psalm 13:1*

The nerve of some people! How dare they talk to God that way! The Bible is supposed to be a book that helps us in our faith, and here we get a psalm written by a man who is fed up with the whole business. This guy is so angry or frustrated over something that he's starting to wonder if God is really there. There are a number of other psalms like this. What are they doing in the Bible?

They must be there because they show a common feeling. Why deny it? Everyone gets frustrated with life. Maybe you've had a bad day, have been picked on, have failed a task, or find yourself without many friends. It makes you wonder if this is such a grand world. God just doesn't seem to be in the picture. Even Jesus had a moment on the cross when he wondered why God had turned his back on him.

Most of us feel ashamed of our frustrations or doubts and try to cover them up. We don't want to ask too many questions about God or religion for fear that we might prove that God isn't there after all. The psalmist wasn't afraid of that. He didn't want a scared faith. He had some questions to ask and some doubts to admit. This didn't cause him to lose faith. In fact, if you read the rest of the psalm, you see that his faith became stronger than ever in the end.

"Seek and you will find," said Jesus. Through all of our frustrations we'll find that God really is here.


Chris was all set for one of the best days of his life. With *two* big treats coming up, it would be his best birthday yet. They were going to travel to the city and watch a pro baseball game from right behind home plate. Then they would stay in a motel and go on to the largest amusement park in the state.

Chris pictured himself rocketing down roller coaster tracks, and he played catch to keep his glove in shape to grab the foul ball that he was sure would come his way. His mind was so busy rehearsing the events only two days away that he didn't notice how weak his stomach felt. Sometimes he felt sweaty and at other times he started

46

to shiver, but he thought it was because he was excited.

The next morning, though, he knew something was wrong. Dad brought out the thermometer and found a high fever. Chris felt so sick he could not even sit up. He stared at the ceiling listening to his dad on the phone trying to find someone who could use the baseball tickets.

Despite his weakness, Chris found enough energy to pound his pillow. *What a time to get sick!* he thought. *Why me? God must have planned this just to get me!* That made no sense, though. God was supposed to love everyone; he didn't play mean little tricks. How could he let a thing like this happen?

Another shudder ran through his body. *Maybe it's all a fake. Maybe he doesn't care about us.* Chris had not thought he could feel any worse, but that idea completely wrecked his spirits. Brooding all day on it, he wasn't able to get the sleep he desperately needed. Finally, when mom came to check on him, he blurted out, "I don't think there is a God." Then, because it sounded like such an awful thing to say, he grew worried. "God wouldn't punish someone as sick as me, would he?"

"You really do feel tough, don't you?" said mom.

Chris closed his eyes, enjoying her cool fingers on his forehead. "Do you ever wonder if there's really a God?"

"I haven't been 100 percent sure every second of my life," she said. "Just like you, I've sometimes felt that the world's only purpose was to make me miserable. That's made me wonder about God."

"That must really get God mad," said Chris.

"I don't know. When you were very small, you used to call out for us in your bed at night. You just wanted to know that someone really was there. It's probably the same with us. Sometimes we have to call out to know that God really is there." Chris nodded and, within seconds, finally fell into a deep sleep.

**Action Idea:** Don't take everything for granted. The Apostle's Creed is a statement of what we believe. Is there something in the creed that you don't understand or that doesn't sound quite right to you? Ask some questions and find out why you should believe it.

*God, there are times when I can't see or feel you here, when the world seems too rotten to imagine that you could be anywhere in it. Please be there when I call out and make my faith stronger than ever.*

# 10 . . . Always So Near

*"And surely I will be with you always, to the very end of the age."*

*Matthew 28:20*

Jesus must have known there would be times when we would have doubts about him. His own disciples were probably some of the most confused people on earth after Jesus' death. Even after they knew he had risen from the dead, they were depressed. They wanted him to always be with them in person.

Not only did Jesus expect doubts, he prepared in advance for them. One of the best tonics for doubt and despair is this verse from Matthew. Jesus promised that he will always be with us, so near that we couldn't get away from him if we wanted to. Even when we are too busy to notice him, he is still close at hand.

The Bible mentions sheep so often that we don't always stop to get a real picture of the animal. Think of a sheep grazing on the range. It doesn't glance up every 10 minutes to make sure there's a shepherd around. It goes about its business, not caring who's watching it and not noticing when it's heading into trouble. The shepherd is the one who does the watching. A shepherd who spots a sheep heading for trouble doesn't wait for the sheep to call. He rushes right in to bring the sheep back.

Jesus compared us to sheep because we, too, wander off into trouble without knowing how we got there. So many powers in the world are stronger than we are that it's natural to be afraid. When we're really in trouble, we need to have God close by. Just look at the verse. He is here, he always has been, and he always will be. And if God is watching over us, is there anything that can harm us?

As their car sped along a winding dirt road, Dennis wondered how he had gotten himself into this jam. He thought back to the filmstrip presentation he had seen on the summer camp. By the time the filmstrip had finished, he could hardly wait to get out into the woods and try some rugged camping. It sounded like all the things he had wanted to do—riding horses, canoeing, and exploring.

But then his friend had backed out because of a family vacation. No one else that he knew had signed up. Suddenly the appeal had faded, and Dennis could see only problems ahead. He was heading into a strange camp, completely alone. Slumping lower in his seat, he thought of the tent he would be pitching. *With six other guys who are all best friends*, he thought. Bad scenes were play-acted in his mind. He was trying to be outgoing, but everyone just ignored him. After awhile, everyone got bored and started picking on him. Everyone else was an expert at camping, and they laughed at his clumsy efforts.

By the time Dennis saw the final sign for the camp, he had worried his stomach into a knot. *No, not already*, he thought as he saw the half-filled parking lot behind the sign. *Why did I ever sign up for this? God, get me through this torture.*

He hadn't meant it as a prayer, but the thought of God sent a small wave of hope through him. *Maybe it really would be awful if it was just me*, he thought. *Why do I always forget about God?* The thought that he wasn't totally alone after all made it easier to get out of the car.

Dad stretched his cramped muscles after climbing out of the car and took a quick look at the camp. "Are you nervous, Dennis?"

"Yep."

"Wish you hadn't signed up?"

Dennis looked out across the valley at the woods and ridges, and the stream winding along the bottom. There must have been 30 horses grazing in a fenced pasture, and there were rows of

51

gleaming canoes stacked near the parking lot. A group of people in camp T-shirts were moving toward him, and they looked friendly. "Who knows? It could even be fun," he said.

**Action Idea:** Do you know of someone who is going through a tough time right now? See what you can do to let the person know that there is someone who is concerned and would like to help.

*Thank you for your promise, Lord. We need to be sure that you are with us. Believe me, it helps to know that!*

# 11 It's Tough to Figure It All Out . . .

*Oh, the depth of the riches of the wisdom and knowledge of God! How unsearchable his judgments, and his paths beyond tracing out!*

*Romans 11:33*

The Old Testament tells the story of a man who had the world's worst losing streak. His name was Job, and he was as good a man as you could find. Unfortunately, being good didn't seem to do him any good. Everything went wrong in his life. He suffered through terrible sicknesses and lost all his money, his house, his job, and his family. His friends only made it worse by telling him that it was all his own fault for having done something wrong in his life. Job knew that wasn't true. Although he was a sinner like everyone else, he had always tried hard to follow God. Why was all this happening to him?

All of our universities, seminaries, and computers have brought us no closer to answering Job's question. There are at least as many baffling questions asked today as there were 1000 years ago, with no hope of any answers. Why do some people have such problems? What does God want me to do next? Why is the world like it is and not some other way? When does God act in our world and when does God leave us to handle things ourselves? Is this church leader right, or is that one?

You may have had many questions of your own that have made your parents or other adults just sigh and shrug their shoulders. When we try to study God, we're getting into an area that's too big for us to master. God is so great and so wonderful, and the world so complicated, that the more we study it, the more we marvel at the unexplained power behind it.

Paul pulled the wad of letters out of the mailbox and flipped through them. One letter was addressed to the whole family and, since Paul rarely got mail, he opened it himself. "Hey, mom! Guess who's getting married?"

Mom looked up from the magazine she was reading. "Did we get a wedding invitation? Well, that must be from your cousin Mary. When is it going to be?"

Paul glanced over the fine script. "On the 30th." Then he saw something that made him stop and read the entire invitation. There was no mistake; it said clearly that it was at St. Paul's Catholic

54

Church. Mary had to be marrying a Roman Catholic, then. Paul wasn't sure what it meant to be Catholic, except that it was different. He had read books and seen movies and news reports that showed some people made a big deal out of it. Some people automatically hated anyone of a different faith.

Paul handed the invitation to mom and hovered around her, waiting for a reaction. But she folded the invitation without saying a word. Finally Paul asked, "Is it alright with Uncle Frank and Aunt Carol that she's marrying a Catholic?"

"Oh, I'm sure they've asked the two kids to talk it all out so they know about any problems that might come up. But we've come a long way on getting along since I was a girl."

"How can we be so different when we're both Christian?" Paul asked.

Mom put aside her magazine. "Different groups have different ideas on how things should be run. Christianity seems to be split among hundreds of groups with their own ways of looking at things. Then you've got hundreds of non-Christian groups with more different thoughts about God."

"It's like a test question, then. There are hundreds of wrong answers but only one right one?"

Mom smiled. "We act that way some of the time. But how likely is it that whenever two people disagree, the same one is always right? Since we're all human, I expect all Christian churches are right on some points and wrong on others. There are probably many right answers to some questions."

"I don't get it," said Paul. "How did we get so mixed up about God?"

Mom flipped open her magazine. "I just read two articles on the economy by two experts in the field. Would you believe one said the opposite of what the other did? When you have a subject that complicated, all you can do is make your best guesses."

"And what bigger subject is there than God?" said Paul.

"Right," replied his mother. "We can't say we've got God figured out. We can just be amazed at how great God must be."

**Action Idea:** Do a little research on another religious faith. Talk to a person from another denomination and find out what is different and what is the same about your faiths.

*God, you wouldn't be so magnificent if it was easy to figure you out. Forgive our pride when we think we have all the answers about you. Help people of different faiths to get along, to learn from each other, and to set aside their differences to work for your kingdom.*

# 12 ... But Some Answers Are Easy

*He has showed you, O man, what is good. And what does the Lord require of you? To act justly and to love mercy and to walk humbly with your God.*
*Micah 6:8*

Thousands of people sweat out exams every year. It's hard enough facing school tests and tryouts for Little League. But when your whole life plan depends upon passing a test, it can really be scary. High school students may be a bundle of nerves as they take a test for getting into college. College students may study all night while everyone else sleeps just in order to pass tests to get into medical school.

It would be tougher yet to pass a test of what God is and what God wants. The questions are so hard that we wouldn't know where to start. We can't begin to understand all there is to know on the subject. There have been stories of people who have climbed the highest mountains in search of a holy man who could tell them what life is about. These desperate attempts always fail.

Fortunately, God has boiled down the vast information to a few basics. He wants to be known by all, not just the most learned scholars. So he says that the deep questions about God and the world may be fascinating, but they aren't necessary.

The prophet Micah says that it's simple to understand what God expects of us: to do what's right, to show kindness, and to love God. Whatever else you want to say about the subject is extra. Jesus used to do the same thing when he talked about God. What are God's commandments? Simple—love God and your neighbor. How are we saved? Simple—believe and be baptized. We will search the rest of our lives to find out all we *want* to know about God. But everything we *need* to know is as plain as can be!

After seeing his friends leave for supper, Russ closed the front door and went to the kitchen. There dad was cooking his speciality—beef stew. "Say, where was Neil today?" dad said, sprinkling in some spices. "I haven't seen him around for a long time, come to think of it."

"We're not the best of friends anymore," shrugged Russ.

"This is runny stuff," said dad. "Could you get me a tablespoon of flour? Neil is such a nice guy. What's wrong?"

"Anyone can be nice," said Russ, scooping out the flour. "Neil was probably too nice. I mean, he never got excited about anything. He never had any plans or ideas. We never went to his house; we always came here."

"That shouldn't have been a problem," said dad. "You usually have enough ideas for a whole crowd."

"Well, it seemed like such a waste of time. Don't you get tired of people like that after awhile?"

Dad stirred the stew without answering. "By the way, someone called today about the nursery at church. Seems like they need a few extra hands around on Sundays. You interested?"

"Yuk!" said Russ. "Those kids just drool all over and cry."

"Alright, take my place in choir and I'll watch the kids this week."

"No thanks, I hate to sing. I'll go to church and Sunday school. That takes enough of my time on Sunday."

The main course was finally ready, and dad shut off the stove. "You're lucky God doesn't use your standard of judging," he said.

"Huh?" said Russ.

"Neil didn't pass your standards because he didn't want to do anything except come over.

Well, you don't seem to be leaping at the chance to do anything for God except show up. You suppose God gets tired of people like that?"

Russ blushed as he thought back on his reasons for not doing anything extra at church. They did sound like excuses Neil would come up with. "I guess God doesn't really ask that much," he admitted. "Oh, alright, I'll help out in the nursery." He looked at dad, who didn't seem quite convinced. Then he broke into a laugh and said, "How about if I get Neil to help? Maybe he's ready for some new ideas."

**Action Idea:** Practice the art of kindness, even with people you aren't especially fond of.

*Lord, I know I've grumbled and complained about doing anything "extra" for you. Forgive me. I want to do what I can for you, especially since you ask so little of me.*

# 13  The Troublemaker . . .

*"Do you think I came to bring peace on earth? No,
I tell you, but division."*

*Luke 12:51*

The young priest, Martin Luther, stood before a
stern group of church officials. Luther's hands and
knees must have been shaking and his heart nearly
breaking his ribs as he thought about the danger he
was in. If he did not take back what he had said about
some church policies, he could be killed. If he would
only back down, all the trouble would go away. But
when the time came, something deep inside Luther
told him that he had to stick with what he really believed. That something was a conscience, and it
caused trouble for Luther and the entire Christian
church.

That little troublemaker, the conscience, has upset the lives of many people. Even the world's greatest peacemakers, those who have won the Nobel Peace Prize, have made many enemies because of their consciences. They *must* do what is right no matter how unpopular. Our consciences don't always put us in danger, but they often make trouble.

It's often easy to cheat, or walk off with something from a store without paying, or to put the blame on another person. Sometimes there's not a chance in a hundred of getting caught. You could do it, and it would be over and forgotten. Or you could just not get involved when someone needs your help, and no one would know the difference.

That's when the troublemaking conscience shows up. When a conscience has been strengthened through faith in God, it doesn't care if it causes trouble or makes people uncomfortable. It insists on doing what is right in God's sight even if it upsets the smooth pace of life.

"It's going to be a hot one today," said Barry as he jumped into the back of the truck with the other kids. "It's a good thing we start so early."

Picking raspberries wasn't a fun job, but he hadn't been able to find another way to earn money. When the truck reached the patch, he jumped off and waited until the others had chosen their rows. Then he and the two who usually worked near him spaced themselves down the end row

and began picking. Barry popped a few raspberries in his mouth, but by this time he had grown
tired of them.

This row wasn't as thick with fruit as he had
hoped. Barry frowned as he realized he would fall
short of his goal for the week. It would take another morning, maybe two, before he earned the
$50 he needed to pay for soccer camp.

As he stood in line at the end of the morning
waiting for his weekly paycheck, he rubbed the
scratches on his arm. Finally Barry reached the
table and picked up his check. It was for $14 more
than he had expected! Studying the attached
statement, Barry found the mistake. He had only
been in the patch a short while on Tuesday, yet
they had credited him with 30 boxes for that day.
"I'll bet it was really three," Barry chuckled.
"Hey, that means I'm done here. I've got the
$50!" For the first time, he enjoyed the ride home
in the back of the truck. He knew how sloppily
they kept records at that place. They wouldn't
catch the error even if they bothered to check.

Barry didn't think any more about it that night.
It wasn't until the next day that it occurred to him
that something might not be right. "But they
make a bundle of money on us kids," he thought.
"If they were paying what they should, I'd have
more than $50 anyway."

But the extra $14 kept coming back to haunt
him. He tried to talk himself out of going back,
especially since the weather had turned beastly

64

hot and he could hardly stand the thought of going back into the patch. Finally, though, he had to admit that he would have been furious if it was he who had been cheated out of $14.

On Monday morning he waited on the curb as the truck slowed to a stop. With the uncashed check in his pocket, he climbed into the dark, dirty vehicle again. *Easy come, easy go*, he thought as he pulled out the check. *Well, in a morning and a half I'll have the money—free and clean!"*

**Action Idea:** Can you remember a time when you got away with something you shouldn't have? Or when you were given something you didn't deserve? Even if it was years ago and has been comfortably forgotten, it is never too late to make it right.

*Dear Jesus, it's tempting to take the easy way out. Keep my conscience alive and strong so that I don't slip into comfortable wrong actions.*

# 14 . . . Who Brings Peace

*"Peace I leave with you; my peace I give you. I do not give to you as the world gives. Do not let your hearts be troubled and do not be afraid."*

*John 14:27*

What does Jesus have in mind? Is he bringing peace or isn't he? If he's just going to upset our lives, the church, and the whole world, as we saw in the last chapter, why even mention peace? And what does the record show about Jesus and peace? Even when he was here on earth there was fighting going on. He promised his disciples peace, and look what happened to them. They lived through rough times.

Did the disciples find peace? We pray for peace more than we pray for anything. Do we get it? Or is this just another one of those things about God that we can't understand?

Peace is one of those words that can mean several things. Maybe one day God will see to it that fighting stops on earth. But Jesus tells us that the peace he is talking about may be a little different.

Think of driving a car in the lonely north woods late at night. You're getting tired, and you can't find the turn that you were told to look for in your directions. After following a bumpy, winding dirt road for miles, you come to a fork in the road. You can go right or left, but not straight ahead. What do you do? At this point it doesn't matter how much food, games, money, equipment, friends, or muscles you have. It doesn't matter much how well you get along with people. You would trade a great deal to be able to know which is the right road.

Jesus brings the peace of knowing the right road. Our lives may not always be smooth, and we may not always know where we will end up. But there is tremendous peace and calm in knowing that when we do what God asks, we are being the people God intends us to be.

Steve sat on the couch watching his grandma twist the yarn into shapes with her knitting needles. Soon his gaze slipped from the needles and yarn to the hands that were working with them. They were old hands, so old that the skin seemed a see-through film over bulging blood vessels and bones. Grandma couldn't knit the way she used to. She no longer saw or heard well, and Steve knew that when she wanted to get up from the couch, he would have to help her out of the soft cushions. Suddenly he felt very sorry for her.

"Grandma, I hope you live for a long, long time."

She laughed in a cracking voice. "You can't expect that much time left when you get to be my age, Steven."

Her laughter puzzled him, and he wondered if he could actually continue on this forbidden subject of death. "Do you ever think about dying, grandma?".

"Often," she nodded, still undisturbed.

"Does it scare you to think about it?"

"It used to," said grandma. "But there's not much to be scared of that I can see. The worst part is thinking I won't be able to see you grow up."

"I'll miss you too," said Steve, sadly.

"Come on, you haven't lost me yet," said grandma. "I'm still here."

"I hate to think about death," said Steve with a shudder.

"I'm ready for it every night," said grandma firmly.

"How come it doesn't bother you?"

"Well, the Lord and I go back a long ways together. I suppose there are things I would change if I had it all to do over again, but that's all been settled. I may not have been the best person, but God saved me anyway. So I figure I'll be in good hands when it's time for me to go." She snipped

69

the end of a tangled ball of yarn and flipped it to Steve. "Wind that for me, will you?"

Steve agreed. "Age does have some privileges."

**Action Idea:** Talk to a grandparent or a great-grand-parent about their lives and about how they've changed over the years. Find out what it was like to be young many years ago and what it is like to be old now.

*O God, we pray again for peace, as we have so often. At the same time, though, we work against peace by arguing, fighting, and worrying. Give us the power to control our fears and our anger.*

# 15 Let God Do His Work . . .

*So is my word that goes out from my mouth: It will not return to me empty, but will accomplish what I desire and achieve the purpose for which I sent it.*
*Isaiah 55:11*

There's no way to reason with some people. You go out collecting money for UNICEF and you get excuses and doors closed on you. When you're done you wonder what good your couple of dollars will do for a project that needs millions. You're nice to your sister and she just crabs at you. You smile at a store clerk and she snaps at you. You go Christmas caroling at a retirement home and people don't look up from the puzzle they are doing. You have a caring teacher trying to help you learn and some kid ruins the class period with his smart mouth.

What's the use? Where is all your work getting you? The world seems a mess, and even your efforts to help your own corner of it seem to fall flat sometimes. After awhile, it seems you're trying to paint a building with a toothbrush. Why even try?

The prophet Isaiah wants to give you some hope. People around him must have been discouraged by those who wouldn't listen to reason. Isaiah reminds them, and us, who is really in charge. Take the most stubborn person you know; could he really resist God? Think of the most hopeless task you know. Is it too big for God to handle?

Isaiah reminds us that God's work can be done even though we don't see the results. We can touch people without realizing it, and it may be years before it has any effect. But God's will is at work. Leave the worrying to God.

Gary's hands were sticky, so he wiped his forehead with his arms. They had been there since before 6:00 A.M., working to get the Easter breakfast ready. It had been Gary's dad who had insisted they do it up with all natural ingredients and nothing cheap. It had taken a frantic pace, but the smells of pancakes, bacon, eggs, juice, and coffee signaled that all was almost ready.

Gary checked the clock. The service should have ended by now, so breakfasters would be streaming down the stairs at any moment. "Could you check the coffee, Gary, and see if it's ready?" his friend Barry said.

Gary left his griddle and dashed to check the two percolators. Something was wrong! One of the two pots was still cold to the touch. The switch was on and the plug was in, but nothing had happened. "This one hasn't even started!" he yelled.

Frustrated, Dad threw a towel against the wall. "Must be a faulty outlet! Try it over here. Some will just have to wait for their coffee; there's nothing we can do about it."

Seeing his pancakes were ready for flipping, Gary forgot about the coffee. A crowd had formed around the serving area, and Gary fought the urge to flip the pancakes before they were ready just to keep up with the demand.

Suddenly a woman burst in through a back door, clutching a coffee pot. "Where's the coffee? Everyone's run out," she snapped.

"Sorry, there was a bum outlet so we're a little behind on that," said his dad.

"You mean that one?" the woman pointed at the offending outlet. "That thing hasn't worked for weeks. You have to use a different one."

"We know that now," said Barry's dad calmly.

Finally the woman grumbled her way out of the kitchen, and Gary turned angrily to his dad. "What's the use trying to please anyone? After all the work we put in, all we get is gripes. People are hopeless and this church is hopeless! See if they ever get me to do anything again."

"That's the kind of world it is," said the man next to him. "You have to get used to it. You can't expect to change people."

"You're forgetting one thing," dad said. "This is God's world, and I think he means to keep making it better. You can't quit doing your job because you can't see progress."

A smiling face popped in the door. "Best breakfast I've had in 25 years!"

Dad nudged Gary. "Of course little rewards like that make it easier," he said.

**Action Idea:** Don't avoid people just because they are unpleasant. Don't back away. Answer grumbling and even insults with positive statements. Spread cheer around and leave it to do its work.

*Where hatred and anger burn out of control, may your will be done.*
*Where greed and selfishness freeze heart and soul, may your will be done.*
*Where hunger and pain sweep across the land, may your will be done.*
*Extend to all your great healing hand, and may your will be done.*

# 16 . . . And Let's Do Ours

*Then I heard the voice of the Lord saying, "Whom shall I send? And who will go for us?" And I said, "Here am I. Send me!"*

*Isaiah 6:8*

The danger in remembering how powerful God is comes when we decide God can do everything by himself. Some Christians in the early church were so sure that Jesus was coming again soon that they quit their jobs and lounged around waiting for it to happen. They must have thought that God put us on the earth only to be spectators, to cheer him on while he showed off his mighty tricks.

This verse from Isaiah reminds us not to sit back and let God do it all. God uses people to spread his love, and it's a job that is never finished. God has

75

plenty of plans waiting for someone willing to carry them out.

Isaiah tells us how he happened to start preaching and writing about God. He had a vision or a dream in which he heard God asking for volunteers. He could have said that he was busy or that he just wasn't ready for that kind of thing. Moses, for example, tried to beg off at first when he heard God's call. The prophet Jonah tried to escape God's call by sailing out of the country as fast as he could. But Isaiah's answer must have made God feel warm all over. Like a student begging for his teacher to call on him in class, Isaiah jumped up and said, "Let me do it!"

Sure, God can do everything. But if he made all the moves himself, life would be no more meaningful than if he were playing house or moving toy soldiers around. And if we expect God to handle every problem that comes up, without any effort on our part, we are treating him as if he were just a servant here to make our lives better. It's our world, too, and there is much we can do to help.

As they watched the ragged-looking girl duck inside a broken back door, Pat poked his friend and said, "There's something strange about her."

"You're not kidding!" Tony said. "You should live two doors down from them like I do. I could tell you stories about them you wouldn't believe!"

That sounded exciting. "Come on, start talking!"

76

"My parents won't speak to them," said Tony. "They say they're ruining the neighborhood. When that girl came to our door once, my dad told her to get out of our yard."

"Why?" asked Pat. "What's wrong with them?"

"Listen to them sometime. Even her three-year-old brother swears all the time. And they're dirty and always wrecking property."

Pat stared at the house as if it were haunted. He wondered what went on in that place. "Don't their parents get after them?"

"The mom's only 24, and she's divorced."

Pat thought Tony was pulling his leg. "How could the mom be only 24? That girl must be eight years old."

"That's what I heard," shrugged Tony.

Pat rushed home to tell his mom the news about the family. "I know they must be brats," he said, "but you have to feel sorry for them. What's going to happen to those kids?"

"Good question," said mom. "If no one cares for them at home and all they see from neighbors is hate, what chance do they have?"

"What would you do if they lived by us?" said Pat, frowning.

"I hope I would be a little nicer," sighed mom. "But I know it's hard to have neighbors like that."

"Maybe God can do something," Pat said. "Maybe we can just ask God to watch over them."

77

Mom finished drying her hair and looked at the mess in the bathroom. "Is there a job you hate worse than cleaning the bathroom?"

Pat made a face. "No, that's the worst."

"We're willing to do what God wants as long as the work is easy. But when something tough comes along that looks like hard work, we set that aside for God. It's kind of like having God do the dirty work like the bathrooms and storm windows."

"I suppose you're right," Pat said nervously. "But what can we do?"

"If Jesus lived next door, he would probably drop in on them."

"Would he offer to give them a ride to Sunday school?" smiled Pat.

"I'll bet he would. Is it worth a try?"

**Action Idea:** Is there someone in your neighborhood, at school, or at church who seems lonely or who gets left out of things? Make a point to talk to that person in a kind way and try to get them included in activities.

*God, we don't have to look long or far before we find someone who could use help. Don't let those chances slip by. If I can make a difference, give me the strength to at least try.*

# 17   It's All in the Mind . . .

*Hold on to instruction, do not let it go; guard it well, for it is your life.*

*Proverbs 4:13*

Advice is like criticism: most people think it is more blessed to give it than to receive it! Those who are always giving advice are seen as busybodies. They enjoy sticking their noses into other people's business and telling them how to live. Of course that gets us upset. It's not much fun to be around those who always think they know better than you.

Yet if you look closely, people seem to need advice. Some of the bestselling books are the "how to" books that give advice on everything from gardening to making money. Advice columns are popular in newspapers. That's because we like to learn from those who have already gone through the problems we are facing.

The book of Proverbs is an advice book. It's written by the wisest men of that time, in hopes that younger people will learn from them. Most of their advice is as valuable today as it was when Proverbs was written. One of the main bits of advice that Proverbs gives is to use your mind to learn all that you can.

The writers of Proverbs knew that it's tempting to waste time and ignore schoolwork when you are young. Other things seem more important. But when they grew older and saw their time slipping away, they wished they could have those wasted moments back. There is always more to learn about God and his world and never enough time in which to study it. Proverbs was written especially for people like you, in hopes that you will use the mind that God has given you to learn.


"Aaaaaah!" Greg exploded as he scribbled through the wrong answer on his page so hard that he snapped the pencil lead and tore a hole in the paper.

"Could you use some help?" dad asked.

Greg slammed his book shut. "Who cares about this stuff anyway? Math is a waste of time. What do I need math for if I'm going to be a police officer?" He sneered at his whole stack of books from school. "What do I need any of this stuff for? Boring, boring, boring!"

"I'm sorry you feel that way," dad said.

80

"It must be nice for you being out of school," Greg went on. "You don't have to worry about classes or tests or studying any more."

Dad opened his mouth to say something and then thought better of it. Finally he said, "Can this be any harder work than lifting weights like I saw you do last night? That's what *I* would call hard work."

"That's different," said Greg. "Those are supposed to make me strong."

"I don't understand," dad said. "I've known many police officers, but I can't think of one who's ever had to lift weights in the line of duty."

"You're being silly," Greg snorted. "Those exercises build up muscles, and you can use muscles for more than just lifting weights."

"Sounds good," nodded dad. "Have you got exercises that build up the whole body?"

"Most of it," answered Greg.

"How about the brain? Any exercises for that?"

When Greg didn't answer, dad said, "Isn't that what school work is for? Not so that you can do these problems perfectly, but so that your brain is in shape for other things. You've got hundreds of decisions to make each day, and more and more of them come your way as you get older. How are you going to be in shape to make the right choices in life if your mind isn't in shape?"

"I never thought of this as exercising," Greg said. "I guess it doesn't make much sense to exercise all but the most important part of the

81

body." He looked up suspiciously at his dad. "You don't go to school, though. How do you keep in shape?"

Dad squeezed him on the shoulder. "Trying to keep up with kids like you is a pretty good workout."

**Action Idea:** Think of a person you admire very much. It could be someone famous or a person in your community. Find that person's address (if it's a famous person, the library can help) and write a letter to him or her. Ask for the best advice they could give based on their own childhood.

*Almighty God, when you asked King Solomon what he wanted more than any other gift in the world, he chose wisdom. Make that my first choice as well.*

82

# 18  . . . Which Is Part of the Body

*Do you not know that your body is a temple of the Holy Spirit, who is in you, whom you have received from God? You are not your own; you were bought at a price. Therefore honor God with your body.*
*1 Corinthians 6:19-20*

The last chapter had a special message for the young; this time we have a verse that seems to be aimed more at adults. We're talking about the body, and adults are the ones most often out of shape. They have more bad habits that wear down their health and usually have more trouble keeping a healthy weight.

But Paul is talking about more than physical health in this verse; he has also brought up the subject of

83

sex. Does it seem strange for someone to be lecturing adults about sex? Don't adults usually have all the answers and kids all the questions?

Paul says here that taking care of the body includes a good attitude about sex. Adults often fail at that too. But it's important for both young and old to hear that, because habits can start early and they can last a lifetime. Having respect now for our own bodies and for others' can prevent problems later.

Suppose you worked hard to make a present for someone you love. You tiptoed to the basement whenever you could to work on your own special design. Then, when you gave the person the present, he or she just laughed about it, or gave it away. You'd be hurt deeply because no one cared about the time or effort or love that you put into it.

That's what Paul is getting at here. God made our bodies, and it's an amazing job of workmanship. How do we treat a valuable gift like that? What can we do to show the most respect for God's work?

It had not been far from Tom's thoughts since Wayne had given him the news at noon. Wayne had found a magazine left in a clump of bushes back behind the dump on the edge of town. It was the kind of magazine that Tom had heard much about but had never seen. In fact, he had never thought he would see one.

When school was over he sneaked out to the garage and waited. When he poked his head around the corner of the garage, he saw his two friends racing down the alley. Wayne was carrying a brown bag, and Chuck was puffing in an effort to keep up with him.

"Come on in here," Tom whispered when they drew close. "There's enough light back in the corner up on top of the camping gear."

Wayne pulled out the comic books that were covering up his main prize and found the magazine. He quickly flipped through to find the pages with glossy color photographs of naked women. He paid special attention to the blonde featured in the centerfold. "This is great!" he said. All three boys giggled and made jokes as they pored over the pictures page by page.

"Look at this!" Chuck started to say when Tom heard a noise that sent a jolt through him like electricity. The automatic garage door opener was whirring into action.

"She's not supposed to be home until supper," Tom whispered hoarsely. As the car drove into the garage, Wayne stuffed all his magazines back in the paper bag, and he and Chuck scurried out into the alley.

"What have you been up to?" asked mom, jiggling the car keys.

Tom knew his face was burning red. Ashamed and confused, he finally croaked out, "Just some magazines."

"You mean 'adult' magazines? X-rated?"

"What's so bad about it?" he asked stubbornly. "Lots of men read those. And there are pictures like that in the art institute."

"*You* must think there's something wrong," mom said. "All three of you looked as guilty as anyone I've ever seen."

As they walked toward the house, Tom hung his head. "I thought you always said sex was good and healthy."

"What if I found you doing something with my best china *that I didn't like*?" she asked. "Something like feeding the dog."

"Or mixing paint on it? Or playing Frisbee?" Tom said.

Mom shuddered. "You certainly have the idea. Well, I think about sex the same way. It's beautiful and important for special occasions. But it has to be treated special, with respect. Snickering through dirty magazines or cheap jokes is—"

"Like playing Frisbee with your best china?" finished Tom.

"Exactly."

**Action Idea:** Pay close attention to TV shows, movies, commercials, and advertisements in magazines and newspapers. How often is sex used to get your interest? How often is it used in a way that shows respect for sex and for people?

*Lord, help me shape my attitudes now so that sex can always be a wonderful thing, so that when I think of sex I don't think of something seedy or dirty but of God's important gifts.*

# 19 It All Happened So Long Ago . . .

*And when he had given thanks, he broke it and said, "This is my body, which is for you; do this in remembrance of me."*

*1 Corinthians 11:24*

They don't come out with new and improved versions of the Bible. Sure, there are many new translations, but the books and the stories in the Bible are the same. It's been a long time since anyone added any books to the Bible. So when we read it, we're looking into things that happened thousands of years ago. Many of the places and nations in the Bible have been covered by sand for centuries.

Sometimes it seems we spend more time studying what happened in Bible times than we do looking at our own times. Why are we always looking back in

time? If the people in the Bible were to come back to life now, they wouldn't believe this is even the same planet that they once lived on. So what do they have to do with us?

Jesus says in this verse that it is important to look back. He is talking about Communion, an old ceremony that we go through many times each year. We do it to remember Jesus, so we don't forget how important he is. Some people remember things by using tricks such as tying a string around a finger. Jesus came up with a way that works even better.

By taking a special meal of bread and wine, our minds can go back to Jesus' time. We can picture the room where Jesus and his disciples huddled for a last supper. We can hear the chairs scrape, smell the bread, see the flickering candles. When we can see all this, we remember that Jesus is real, that he did take this supper with his disciples, that he did go through the horror of Good Friday and the joy of Easter. It's something worth remembering.

Never having been in a play before, Ted felt as out of place on the stage as a giant wart. When the scene was over, he braced himself to hear what he knew the teacher would say.

"Ted, I'm hearing you loud and clear. That's no problem, but we need to have more expression from you. You have to act more like a Pilgrim and less like Ted Wills."

Ted scowled, "But I don't know how to be a Pilgrim," he said. "I don't know any Pilgrims, and I've never seen one."

The teacher rubbed her chin, trying to think of a way to explain. "You have to try to imagine what it would have been like. They had many hardships in those days. Can you think of what it would feel like if life were that rough for you?"

Ted spread his arms in despair. "I *know* they had it rough, but I just don't know how to act."

This time the teacher turned and pulled a book from under a stack of papers. "There's a section in there, page 50, that describes very well what the Pilgrims went through. Why don't you look through that at home tonight?"

That evening Ted opened the book and started to skim the chapter on Pilgrims. He could hardly believe all the troubles they had, and within a page he was carefully reading every word. The book made it easy to imagine how scared they were; so few of them in a new world they knew nothing about. Their own friends and family were dying from diseases they couldn't cure. What little food they had at the end of winter was rotten. Ted got depressed just reading it.

Then when some friendly Native Americans helped them out, things improved. What a relief it must have been to have a great harvest and to know that, at least this year, there would be something to eat during the cold months. By the time he finished reading, Ted still didn't think he could act, but at least he could try and picture how a real Pilgrim would say those lines.

The Pilgrim episode came back to Ted during Holy Week. He had always wondered about Holy Week and especially about Good Friday. It seemed to be so gory, going through the whole story every year.

But he remembered the play and how important it had been to feel what had gone on in Pilgrim times. This Good Friday depressed Ted more than any he remembered because it all seemed so real to him. When Easter morning came, though, it was easy to feel the relief and the joy that came with the empty tomb. He even found himself smiling most of the day. *So that's what happened on Easter,* he thought.

**Action Idea:** Try to picture, in detail, what Jesus looked like. What do you think his favorite color might have been? Favorite food? What did his voice sound like? Carry that picture in your mind when you go up for Communion or for an altar blessing next time.

*Help me remember, Lord, that the Bible is more than a storybook, that great things happened 2000 years ago that changed the world and my life. Thank you for being real and for helping us to understand you through the sacrament of Communion.*

# 20 . . . But You Ain't Seen Nothin' Yet!

*"And if I go and prepare a place for you, I will come back and take you to be with me that you also may be where I am."*

*John 14:3*

A popular hotel chain advertises that you will get no surprises when you reserve one of their rooms. Everything will be exactly as you expect it. Jesus takes the opposite approach when it comes to reserving rooms for us. He doesn't give us a very clear picture of what we're going to get. About all we know is that it will be a surprise; it will be different from anything we've ever imagined. And one more thing— he also guarantees that we're going to like it!

Jesus talks in this verse about heaven. It was one of his favorite subjects, judging by how often he

93

talked about it. We still talk about heaven today, although we have little idea of what the details are. Many questions pop into our minds: What is it like? How will we keep from getting bored? What will we look like? Will we be the same age as our parents or will they still be older than we are? We're so used to worrying about the future that we can even get ourselves into a stew over what heaven is like. We'd rather not think about what is to come in our lives. It's safer to dwell on the "good old days."

When Jesus talked about what is to come, though, he was often rubbing his hands in anticipation. He says that the "good old days" haven't come yet, that our best memories won't compare with what is to come. What he has done is give us hope.

Have you ever watched a football team that has fallen out of the championship race? Sometimes these teams can't give out their usual effort, and they get blown away in their final games by their opponents. Without the hope of a playoff spot, they have trouble doing their job.

Jesus has given us something to go for, so that even though we may face some hard times, we can still have hope. We know that when we reach the end, it's going to be good.


"Better head home, Lee. Rain's coming," called Roger.

Seeing the thick, black clouds sweep in from the west, Lee agreed. "Let's cut through the quarry; it's faster. Just watch your step. There are some deep drop-offs in there."

94

"Don't worry," said Roger. But halfway through the quarry, his foot slipped. He tried to stop his fall by grabbing a rock, but it, too, broke loose and fueled the growing rock slide. Lee saw the slide and the splashes and called down, "Are you OK, Roger?"

Too scared to even scream, Roger looked up towards the voice. Lee seemed so far away atop the sheer cliff. "This water's deep!" he gasped. "Get me out, quick!"

Lee searched for a path down to the water, but there was no way down. "I'll have to run for help. Hang on!"

Roger hated to see him leave, but he knew Lee couldn't get him out without help. For awhile he treaded water, but it began to sap his energy. Several times he tried to cling to an edge of the water hole, but there was no place to get a grip and his hand kept slipping off.

Cold and exhausted, Roger pleaded, "Get back here, please!" He thought he heard voices once, but when no one showed up he felt his strength fading. Out of breath, his muscles numb, he began to sink into the water. "I can't hold on," he thought, and he started to cry as he realized he couldn't last any longer.

But then he heard a droning noise, and then tiny voices. This time it was no mistake. The voices were getting louder! Roger's legs seemed to find a last bit of energy, and he fought his way back to the rocky edge.

"Roger!" screamed Lee.

"I can't last," gasped Roger. A neighbor, Mr. Fowler, quickly tied a rope to his tractor and climbed down to get Roger. The rope was barely long enough, and Mr. Fowler had to stretch to reach Roger's almost limp arm. When he had at last been pulled to safety, Roger huddled in a blanket and tried to get his teeth to stop chattering.

"I thought I was done until I heard you coming. All at once I found some strength that I didn't know I had."

"It's amazing what hope can do," said Mr. Fowler. He pointed to a bright rainbow that had dropped between the clouds. "Isn't that why God sent those? Hope." Roger nodded and shivered. "Wish there would have been an easier way to learn what hope can do."

**Action Idea:** Get out a calendar and mark on it those coming events that you are looking forward to. If you can't think of enough, plan some things to look forward to. Keep those in mind and see if they improve your outlook when you're in a bad mood.

*Lord, I hope to be with you someday. Keep me going in the meantime with a good measure of hope to keep me from getting discouraged.*

# 21 Something Extra for Parents . . .

*"Honor your father and your mother, as the Lord your God has commanded you."*

*Deuteronomy 5:16*

Nearly every child has wondered, at one time or another, why we have a Mother's Day and a Father's Day, but no Children's Day. The standard answer to that has always been "because every day is children's day."

I don't know about you, but I was never very happy with that answer. This verse from Deuteronomy may be a better answer. It may not get us any closer to having a Children's Day, but at least it's something we can understand. There it is, a clear command from God for us to honor our father and mother. It doesn't say anything about honoring kids. There's

97

nothing in the entire Ten Commandments about honoring kids.

What does God have against kids? Nothing. We don't have to feel insulted whenever someone else gets singled out for a compliment. This commandment compliments parents and points out that they have a special role in life. Because of that, we should honor them.

Sometimes it takes a tragedy before we understand what parents and children mean to each other. Some parents who lose children slowly come to realize that the child didn't really *belong* to them. A child belongs to God, and parents are special caretakers. Their job of caring for God's children and bringing them up in a responsible way may be the most important job God gives to anyone.

When God says that parents should be honored, he is saying that children are important. Because children are so important, we should have a special respect for the people whom he has trusted to watch over them.

"That was Uncle Howard," said mom, hanging up the phone. "We're going to drive over to their place tomorrow and stay for the day."

"Oh, no, we're not!" said Dale.

"Just what do you mean by that?"

"I'm not going," Dale insisted. "There's nothing for me to do over there with a couple of girls who sit around and do boring things."

"We're going as a family," mom said firmly. "Your dad hasn't had a chance to see his brother for a long time."

"You can go," Dale said, "but I'm staying home. I hate going there."

"I told Uncle Howard that we're coming," said mom, leaving the room. "I'm not going to stand here and argue with you."

Dale pulled his pajamas off the closet hook and sat on his bed to take off his socks. "It isn't fair," he thought. "No one cares if I suffer the whole day. They better not expect much cooperation from me! They'll wish they paid attention when I said I didn't want to go!" As he finished dressing, he heard his dad come in from the garage. With his bedroom door opened a crack, Dale could hear their conversation.

"This is about the first chance I've had to talk to you in a couple of days," dad said.

"Yes, we've both been too busy. But I think we've got nearly everything crossed off our list. Laundry's done, rolls are made, the car has been tuned up," said mom. "I hated to ask you to go out again, but Dale didn't have any decent pants for tomorrow."

"No problem," dad said. "Will these do?" he asked.

"Perfect," said mom. "Just the color he asked for. Hope they fit."

"It'll sure be good to relax at Howard's tomor-row," dad said. "You know, it's been so long I'm not sure I can find the place. "We've only been there once since they moved."

"Your back's bothering you, isn't it?" said mom. "Lie down on the floor and I'll give you a back rub."

Dale felt a little guilty by the time he was under the covers. His parents really did work hard, and much of that was for him. They didn't gripe about it either, at least not when he was around.

Dale thought back, trying to remember the game that his parents especially like to play. He remembered his mom telling him that they played it often with young couples when they were first married. *Charades, that was it,* Dale thought. *Maybe we can all play that tomorrow at Uncle Howard's.*

**Action Idea:** Even if it isn't near Mother's Day or Father's Day, give your parents a gift. Make it a gift of time, such as a certificate good for so many extra hours of yard work, floor scrubbing, special projects, or cooking.

*Thank you, God, for my parents. These are the things I especially like about them (list as many as you can). The task of caring for the young is such an important one. Help me to always show respect for my parents as they carry out their important task.*

# 22  . . . Something Extra for Children

*"Let the little children come to me, and do not hinder them, for the kingdom of God belongs to such as these."*

*Mark 10:14*

*"Apartment for Rent: No Children or Pets Allowed"*

Signs like that one don't make children feel very important. Sometimes adults act as though children are just a nuisance. When children can learn to act like adults, then they're OK. But until then, children are something you have to put up with, according to some.

It's not likely that Jesus' disciples were mean men who liked to bully children and kick dogs. When they tried to shoo a group of children away, they thought they were doing Jesus a favor. They were certain that Jesus had more important things to do than listen to a bunch of noisy kids. Sometimes our churches do just what the disciples did. Sometimes we try to keep children quiet and out of sight during a worship service. Perhaps we think that we're doing Jesus a favor; that worship is too important to allow children to disturb it.

But Jesus had a big surprise for his disciples. He said that children are not pests. In fact, he told them that they and all adults should learn some lessons from children. One of those lessons was demonstrated at our house a few weeks ago. A little neighbor boy stormed out of our back door, yelling that he would never play with our son again as long as he lived. What's more, he never wanted to see him again! Within a half hour, I found him playing quietly and happily with our son in the basement! Can you imagine what would have happened if an adult had made such hot-tempered remarks? It could leave hatred and bitterness that would last a lifetime. The gift of true forgiveness is only one of many gifts that children bring to God's kingdom.

The State Fair was held clear across the state from the large city in which the Johnson family lived. This was the first time that Ron had ever been to the fair, and he could hardly decide where he wanted to go first. Dad showed him a brightly colored map of the fairgrounds with all the exhibits marked.

"Why don't we go and see the animals first?" Ron said.

102

His older brother Scott hooted. "Come on, it's not like a zoo. These are just plain, ordinary, everyday animals like cows and pigs."

"I wouldn't mind skipping that," agreed dad. "There was a time when I had to work a couple of summers on a farm. I said then that if I never saw another pig in my life it would be too soon!"

Ron hung his head a bit. Suddenly all of those other exhibits didn't interest him; he had wanted to see the animals. Mom noticed his gloomy expression and stopped the other two. "You know, I'm not sure Ron has ever been on a farm. Have you, Ron?" Ron shook his head.

"I never thought of that," said dad. "We moved to the city when he was about two. You've never even been up close to a horse, have you?"

"I've only seen them from a car window."

Dad looked at mom as if he couldn't believe that anyone could have gone this long in life without seeing farm animals. "Well, let's go."

First they found a building filled with cows. Wading through the straw on the floor, he crept as close as he dared to an enormous black bull staring at him through wild eyes. Ron couldn't believe there were so many different kinds of cows. But the highlight for him was when a woman sitting on a three-legged stool offered to show him how to milk a cow by hand. Ron tried, without much luck, and then stood back to watch as his dad proudly took his turn and got streams of milk to spray into the pail.

Then it was on to the pigs. "Hey, Ron, look at this one!" shouted Scott. Ron ran to Scott and saw a hog so huge it seemed the size of a small bull. "I never dreamed they grew so large!" he said.

The Johnsons spent the entire morning with the animals, moving to the horses with their shining flanks, and then to the chickens, turkeys, and sheep. "That time went fast," said dad, looking at his watch. "You really taught me something, Ron. Sometimes we get so grown-up and so used to the way things are that we don't realize how many fascinating things are in the world."

"It sure made a difference watching the animals through your eyes," said mom. "Thanks for keeping us young."

**Action Idea:** Ask your parents what they are most thankful for about you.

*Thank you, Lord, for making room for everyone in your kingdom. We don't have to be old, or rich, or powerful, or intelligent to belong. Thank you for your special love for children. Help me to stay young in my thinking and to help those who are older to stay young too.*

# 23    Quiet on the Set!

*"Be still, and know that I am God."*

*Psalm 46:10*

When you lie in bed tonight, tune your ears to the sounds around you. Notice how the house comes alive at night. The creaking of a floorboard. The ticking of a clock two rooms away. Maybe the wind swishing through the trees. If you press your head against your pillow, you can hear the thumping of your pulse in your ear. Why do you hear these sounds at night and not during the day? Houseboards are resettling and clocks are ticking all day. Your heart has been beating since before you were born. How come you don't hear these sounds during the day?

105

The answer, of course, is that they have been drowned out. Daytime is a noisy time. Cars and machinery fill the air with noise. Voices of family, friends, and teachers, the sounds of radios, razors, footsteps, dogs barking, sirens blaring, doors slamming, and dishes clattering all drown out the quieter noises. Most of the time you could not hear the ticking of a clock in the day even if you listened carefully for it. But get rid of those daytime noises, and suddenly your hearing picks up much, much more.

This psalm tells us that the same thing is true when it comes to hearing God. The busy hustle of life sends noise through our minds. We get so involved in work or play, in dealing with people and problems, in remembering where to be at a certain time, that we don't give God a second thought.

We're likely to find that we don't notice God much in our lives if we don't get some quiet time. Like the ticking of the clock, God's message goes on all the time whether we realize it or not. At some time during the day, we need to drop everything. This time for being still is called meditation. It gives us time to step back from our day-to-day problems long enough to recognize that God is very near.

*They don't let you sit around at this camp,* Carl thought as he scoured the woods for kindling. Besides hiking at least five miles and playing volleyball, Carl had gone swimming twice and spent an hour on the archery range. It was almost dark now, and Carl had to admit he wouldn't mind getting to sleep early this night.

When he returned to the camp, he added his twigs to the loose arrangement of wood shavings in the fire pit. Meanwhile, others stomped larger branches into smaller pieces, and a few carefully chopped wood with axes.

"What are we going to do at the campfire?" Carl asked.

"Haven't had enough for one day, huh?" laughed Kurt, his counselor. "Nothing much tonight. We've been going at a hard pace, so we're just going to have a quiet, peaceful fire."

Carl looked at his friend Darrin. It didn't sound like much fun to either of them. "Might as well cut out early and get in our sleeping bags," Carl whispered to Darrin.

A group of boys cheered as they met the goal of using only one match and no paper to get the fire started. Carl sat on a stump and watched the flames catch hold of the new sticks set on the fire. Before long there was an orange glow deep in the middle of the fire. Carl liked to poke a stick into the center and watch the wood instantly burst into flames. Then he leaned back and watched the smoke curl up to the sky and enjoyed the warmth of the fire against the chilly night air. It occurred to him that no one had spoken for awhile. Yet, tired as he was, he wasn't bored. As he stared into the crackling fire, he thought of his family back home and how good it would be to see them. He felt a little sad thinking back on the week and

107

how quickly the time had gone. But he was thankful that he had had such a wonderful time, and he wanted to remember every detail of the week to save for those winter nights when he was feeling lonely.

Carl found himself thanking God for all kinds of things, and he worried when the fire began to dwindle and no one added any more wood. Somehow it seemed that God had been so near when that fire was going.

"It's getting late, pal," said Kurt. Carl looked around and noticed he was one of the last campers still awake.

**Action Idea:** Some time during each day, take a moment to relax. Sit back and close your eyes and try to let your muscles go limp. Think of a peaceful, cozy setting, whether it's out in nature or in an inviting room. When you feel relaxed and unhurried, let your thoughts drift toward God in the form of a prayer.

*Sometimes we're so busy, Lord, that we think we are getting along without you. We make enough noise to drown out your message, but you are still here. Help us to take time each day to settle down and concentrate on who you are and what you have to say.*

# 24   Let's Hear It for the One Who Made Us!

*Shout for joy to the Lord, all the earth. Serve the Lord with gladness; come before him with joyful songs.*

*Psalm 100:1-2*

It's fitting that we end a book like this with what seems to be the worst case of saying two opposite things. How can the psalms expect us to be quiet, as we saw in the previous chapter, and to be screaming our lungs out at the same time? We can't do both at once. But there is a time for quiet and serious, and a time for loud celebration.

There was a family who had a son stationed with the Marines in a dangerous foreign country. The family got word that the son was missing in action, and they feared the worst. For days they heard nothing new about him, and they had begun to give up hope that they would see him alive again.

Then came a phone call. Their son had been found! He was alive and well! The family went wild, jumping around the room with screams of joy. After hugging and kissing each other, they still needed to let their joy out. They rushed to phones to call close relatives and friends. Then they ran out into the neighborhood to shout their news, and people streamed out of houses to join the celebration. They wouldn't have dreamed of mumbling a solemn word of thanks; they had to shout it.

Compare that with the 10 lepers whom Jesus healed. In spite of the great miracle that had changed their lives, nine of them never even bothered to come back to thank Jesus. It should not have been a time for silence. Where was the joyful noise?

The Revised Standard Version of Psalm 100 puts exclamation points at the end of four sentences in a row. It's an indication that the writer of this psalm could hardly contain his joy and thanks! That kind of thank you must bring a true feeling of pleasure to God. The point is not that we have to shriek and howl and pound drums and clash cymbals to honor God. But we should not be afraid to really praise God for his glorious works.

They couldn't have chosen a worse time to re-draw the school boundary lines. The new boundaries put Todd into a new school, completely cut off from all of his friends. He wasn't thrilled about being the new kid in school. He'd gone through

110

that many years before, and it hadn't been much fun.

"How do I know I'm going to have any friends at this place?" he asked his mom.

"Todd, you've never had any trouble with that before. You've always been able to make friends."

"Yeah, well, you never know," he sighed. That night in his prayers, he had only one request. "Please, God, help me to find some friends at this new place."

Once school actually started, Todd seemed more relaxed. He had a lot going for him: he was nice, good at sports, did well in class, and had a good sense of humor. Before long, he was bringing friends home or calling from a friend's house to say he would be home for supper.

One afternoon he came home with a bruised cheekbone from a rugged football game. "Just an accident," he shrugged when he saw his mom's worried look. "An elbow didn't look where it was going. Nobody really got hurt—just good, clean fun."

"It looks as if you've found what you had hoped to find at your new school," she commented.

"I must live right," he grinned. "Somehow everything has gone so much better than I expected. I hardly miss the other school." He laughed again. "There I was praying for friends, and now I practically have to tell God, 'Enough!' I need time to be home and study."

"And that's because you 'live right'?" asked his mother with a look of mock anger.

"Well, call it an answered prayer. Is that better?"

"I'll accept that," said mom. She cleared her throat. "Isn't there someone you should be thanking?"

Todd looked guilty for a second. "You're right," he said quietly. "I should thank my mother for giving me her wonderful personality." He laughed and dashed off before his mom could give him a pinch. "I can't help being silly when I feel so good! I know you're right, mom. If I can't thank God for today, when can I thank him?"

**Action Idea:** Your church worship service is full of sections of praise and thanksgiving. Next Sunday, be sure to say those sections like you really mean them!

*You're the best, God, and I wish I could give you a hug. It's strange that people used to be afraid of you and thought of you as a very stern master. Thank you for proving that being great means being loving as well as powerful.*